ABSTINENCE, MARRIAGE AND ETC. ...

FAITH BAYS

To order additional copies of this book, contact:
Xlibris
844-714-8691
www.Xlibris.com
Orders@Xlibris.com

Scripture taken from the King James Version of the Bible.

The King James 2000 Bible, copyright © Doctor of
Theology Robert A. Couric 2000, 2003
Used by permision. All rights reserved.

Scripture quotations marked NLT are taken from the
Holy Bible, New Living Translation, copyright © 1996,
2004, 2007. Used by permission of Tyndale House
Publishers, Inc. Carol Stream, Illinois 60188. All rights
reserved. Website

ISBN: Softcover   978-1-6641-5948-8
        EBook   978-1-6641-5947-1

Print information available on the last page

Rev. date: 02/18/2021

ABSTINENCE, MARRIAGE AND ETC. …

MEMORY VERSE: I THESSALONIANS 4: 7
For God has not called us unto uncleanness, but unto holiness.
-King James 2000 Bible

By

Faith Bays

FOREWORD

This book would not have been possible without the experienced training I have received from high school and college professionals; people who work hard in relating and sharing grammatical expertise to eager students. To my philosophers and professors I dedicate this book. I hope I have shared with others a guide that will help them in instructing and organizing Christian youth activities. To share this is a thrilling adventure.

PREFACE

(The revision of Practical Guidance, Love, Sex, and Marriage)

I am so happy to be able to reintroduce my book to the public once again. When I was asked by the publisher of Xlibris to republish, relaunch, re-release and re-introduce my book to public once more I was really surprised. I was delighted about this offer. However, I did not do it because they asked me to. I prayed about it and talked to God about it. I read my book over again. I thought, well I was concise with the children and I was factual.

On a religious network that further led me to believe that God was speaking there was a documentary about an institute in the sixties that did surveys and research on human sexualties which gave no factual proofs of their findings. However, millions copies of their books were sold without a practical hypothesis. My arguments are proofs from the Word of God.

My arguments are not based on human research or surveys. Nor are they long generalized languages. However, I used contextual scriptures from the Bible that speak to that issue. My theories and practices are a concise, and argumental framework for helping one to make a moral decision in life.

I changed the title of my book and the cover photos. My mini biography is placed on the inside of the book rather than the outside. Everything else is the same. My beliefs have not changed about chastity. My heart hurts for the abused children in our world. When they grow up they are so disturbed that it is hard for them to live a normal life. God's grace and love is their only hope, but they need someone to tell them that God cares. You are loved by Jesus.

So, here I go relaunching this project because I feel there is a generation in the 2020's that needs to read these theories and principles. They are mostly all based on the word of God. It is simple for the children and not complex. Children have questions. If we do not give them sound advice from the word of God, they may get it from a peer who wants to harm them and will not tell them the right way to go whenever they wonder about sex, drugs, marriage, abstinence, celibacy, abortion, etc. It is also supported by Jack T. Chick, James Brosnan, NIDA, Parents United, Parents Anonymous and others. I did not leave out the U. S. Department of Health and Human Services.

As a matter of fact, when I taught my book in a workshop in my hometown to high school students, two professional nurses came to support my medical findings. One talked about STDs, the other talked about alcohol and drug abuse. One of them shared how they overdosed on drugs and alcohol while in college and should have died, but God did not let it happen. She shares how God spared her so that she can tell someone else that Jesus loves you and cares.

She shared that her story was in a book she had written. After the workshop, the youths gathered around her wanting to know how to buy her book. So, God has blessed this project in the past and because he is leading me to relaunch again, I believe there will be some youths who will find sound answers to what they are wondering about.

Contents

SUGGESTED USE

This is a four part lesson for youths concerning practical guidance about love, sex and marriage. Suggested use includes a Christian Workshop, 4-H Club meeting, Girl Scouts or Boy Scouts meeting, Bible Study, Tea or Banquet or any helpful youth fellowship.

ABSTINENCE, MARRIAGE AND ETC. ...

MEMORY VERSE: For God hath not called us unto
uncleanness, but unto holiness. I Thessalonians 4: 7
-King James 2000 Bible

LESSON 1 – The Agony

I.   Introduction

II. Sexual Impurities
     A. Fornication (Thessalonians 4: 1-7; I Corinthians 6: 13-20) B. Lasciviousness
     (Eph. 4: 17-23; II Corinthians 12: 21)
     C. Lust (II Timothy 2: 22; I Peter 2: 11)

III. Sexually Communicable Diseases
     A. Syphilis
     B. Gonorrhea
     C. Aids
     D. HIV

IV. Some Tragedies of Premarital Sex
    A. Unwanted Pregnancies
    1. Results
        a. Marriage?
        b. Abortion?
        c. College education detained?
    2. Assistance
        a. Seek God in prayer
        b. Counseling from an adult Christian

V. Other Tragedies of Premarital Sex
    A. Addictive or Habitual Promiscuity (Romans 1: 24-32)
    B. An Unfavorable Reputation

INTRODUCTION:

In ancient times women were viewed as men's property, good for bearing children and not much more. But marriage is a crucial choice that should be made with great care. Sex ought to be saved for the long-lasting productive joy of marriage and the husband render unto the wife due benevolence; and likewise also the wife unto the husband. The husband and wife should not deprive each other of sexual enjoyment except by mutual consent and for a time. Young people growing up in a godly family should be given practical guidance and advice about love, sex and marriage. For so often a lack of parental counseling and caution have caused many young people to make careless mistakes in courtship and marriage, that can leave a scar or wound in their lives; which can only be healed through the process of time as well as through seeking God in prayer.

I. Sexual Impurities

Fornication is illicit or unlawful sexual intercourse between unmarried individuals. In the 4th chapter of Thessalonians, the Apostle Paul exhort the Thessalonians to live godly and pure and to keep clear of all sexual sins so that you will marry in holiness and honor not in lustful passion. For God has not called us to be dirty minded and full of lust (evil desires) but to be holy and clean. If anyone refuses to live by these rules he is not disobeying the rules of men but of God who gives his Holy Spirit to you. When you accept Christ your attitudes and thoughts must all be constantly changing for the better. Lasciviousness, which is excess unrestrained evil desires and lusts, should be crucified along with all the other sins of the old evil nature. Run from anything that gives the evil thoughts that young people often have, but stay close to anything that makes you want to do right. Have faith and love and enjoy the companionship of those who love the Lord and have pure hearts.

II. Sexually Communicable Diseases

"How could this happen to me?" thought Janice. "I am a nice girl. I've only had sex just once and I caught VD!" "How can I tell my parents?" Janice is an example of many young people who engage in premarital sex without understanding or knowing what God says about chastity and pureness from evil lusts and desires. Below is a list of some communicable diseases terms that we all should be familiar with. Who knows, sooner or later you may find yourself in a position like Janice. At such a moment of great crisis our world seems to crumble apart. God seems distant and silent. Fear brings hopelessness and despair. To have faith and trust in God will give you strength and the courage you need to confront your parents.

1. Syphilis: A venereal infection, caused by the Treponema Palladium epirochete; it is transmitted by sexual contact or through the placenta. Symptoms occur in stages; primary stage: Chancre filled with spirochetes, most often in anal or genital region, but can occur elsewhere; secondary stage: malaise, nausea, vomiting, fever, bone and joint pain, rash, and mouth sores; third staged: soft tumor(gummas) that ulcerates and then heals, leaving scars; they may form anywhere in the body and may or may not be painful.[1]

2. Gonorrhea: Common venereal disease caused by the bacterius Neisseria gonorrhoeae and transmitted through contact with an infected person. Symptoms include painful urination and burning itching and pain around the urethra and in women the vagina.[2]

3. Aids: Serious, often fatal condition in which the immune system breaks down and does not respond normally to infection. The disease became epidemic in the early 1980s, affecting almost exclusively male homosexual.[3]

4. HIV: Human Immunodeficiency Virus is the virus caused by Aids. No drug has yet proved effective against HIV.[4]

---

1 Mikel A. Rothenberg, M.D. and Charles F. Chapman, Dictionary of Medical Terms. (Barron's Education Series Inc., 1989), 429
2 Ibid., p.195
3 Ibid., p.7
4 op.cit.

I. A. Some Tragedies of Premarital Sex

Premarital sex can cause unwanted pregnancies, which sometimes results in an early marriage or an unwanted marriage that does not contain the one emotional quality that is needed to be sustained and that quality is love. Abortion is a very debatable topic because of the different aspects that lies behind one reasons for such a choice. Some reasons people give includes: rape, bad health on the part of the mother, mentally disturbed persons, too young, I don't want to have children, etc. But the Bible clearly states in Revelation 21: 8 that murders shall have their part in the lake which burneth with fire and brimstone. A child conceived in the womb means just as much to God as the one who is in this world already. I feel that a little baby inside its mother has the rights to grow and live to its complete and full term. Only those who want to be justified in committing sins are the only ones who are always striving, debating, and questioning God's people about different subjects like abortion issues that are so clear and easily to be understood. If young mothers feel that they are not capable of raising a child, then giving that child up to adopted parents who will provide the love, care and financial support that the child needs is a better choice than abortion.

Having one's education interrupted because of an unwanted pregnancy doesn't mean that you should give up your career goal. After you have your child go to God in prayer seek the advice and counseling of an adult Christian and remember the words or the Apostle Paul in Philippians 4: 13, KJV – "I can do all things through Christ which strengtheneth me."

B. Other Tragedies of Premarital Sex

One of the most important problems to young people is the control of the sexual urge until they can be suitably and happily married. When young unmarried people wants to have sex before marriage they should be given certain facts about premarital sex that will help them to understand why they should hold in check their sexual urge or desire while they go through professional school, and make a position for themselves so that they can marry and

find a home. First, at least in the case of young women is the danger of injury to reputation which may seriously interfere with their life work; secondly, sexual relations indulged in on a purely physical plane gives little pleasure. Such relations leave only feelings of frustration and vague disgust for that person once the sexual urge has been appeased (II Samuel 13: 1-20). Therefore, habitual sexual relationship even if it's temporary and secretive is never going to give you the wholesome physical and emotional basis or values that you will find only in marriage. By no means however should your love for an individual be restrained to the point whereas you do not know how to express yourself when you are confronted with true love and not just merely physical attraction. It has been said that love repressed does strange things. It sometimes disrupts lives.

ABSTINENCE, MARRIAGE AND ETC. …

MEMORY VERSE: For God hath not called us unto uncleanness, but unto holiness. I Thessalonians 4: 7
-King James 2000 Bible

LESSON 2 – The Ecstasy

I. Sex Undefiled

    A. In Marriage Only (I Timothy 5:14; Proverbs 5:18-19)
    B. Courtship? (Ruth 3:7-11; I Corinthians 7:36-37)

II. A Good Thing (Proverbs 18: 22; Genesis 24:67)

III. First Love (Esther 2:17; Genesis 29: 18-20)

ABSTINENCE, MARRIAGE AND ETC. …

MEMORY VERSE: For God hath not called us unto
uncleanness, but unto holiness. I Thessalonians 4: 7
-King James 2000 Bible

THE ECSTASY

I. Sex Undefiled

I believe that sex between intelligent, sincere, married persons can reach great ecstasies; if there is a real honorable, spiritual love and a sincere desire to make a union succeed. Marriage is commended by the Apostle Paul in I Timothy 5:14 for younger women so that the enemy will have no opportunity for slander. Proverbs instructed the young men in Proverbs against unfaithfulness in marriage and having sex with different people (Proverbs 5: 15-21). He tells them to rejoice in the wife of their youth. Let her charms and tender embrace satisfy you. Let her love alone fill you with delight. Society now have abused the union that God intended to be between a husband and his wife so badly that I feel the Christian parents cannot reinforce enough cautions, warnings and advice to their children on the danger of sex during courtship. Ruth, a woman who took the iniative by God help wanted Boaz to be the one who would care for her and her mother-in-law; so she waited until dark and at her mother-in-law's request located the place where Boaz slept and laid down at his feet. When Boaz awoke and found her, he didn't have to be told what was on her mind. She wanted him for a husband. Flattered he didn't let another sun set before making the legal arrangements for marriage. So girls there is nothing wrong with taking the iniative if you are being led by God to do so. However, don't become over zealous and overly aggressive because this will

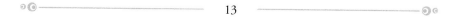

take away from your Christian woman's spiritual adornments which are modesty, meekness and humbleness.

II. A Good Thing

God values love between a man and a woman. God also honors the marriage between two saved individuals who are in love. That's why Solomon wrote in Proverbs, he who finds a wife finds what is good and receives favor from the Lord. A good wife (or husband, we can assume) will make or break her partner's life. Her duties lay the foundation for her family's welfare (Proverbs 14: 1). Married partners should rejoice and be captivated by their love for each other. When Rebekah was brought to Isaac she took her veil and covered herself. Because she knew that betrothed couples were not to have any physical contact until marriage. After Isaac's servant had told him all he had done. Isaac brought Rebekah into the tent of his mother, Sarah, and he married Rebekah. So she became his wife, and he loved her. Isaac at long last had found his good thing.

III. First Love

Many waters cannot quench love; rivers cannot wash it away. Songs of Solomon 8: 7

Plenty of people are shocked to find an explicit love song in the Bible, complete with exotic lyrics. But Songs of Solomon is exactly that. It shows no embarrassment about lover's enjoyment of each other. The lovers love to look at each other. They love to tell each other what they feel. This love is tender filled with delight, natural. You sense no shame or guilt; you feel that God is with the two as they love. The lovers in this song act as equals. Both woman and man take the iniative in praising each other. They don't flirt or play games: they say what they mean. Yet they show caution and dignity in their love. While at the peak of joy, the lovers repeatedly warn others not to stir up love prematurely. Because these lovers recognize the explosive side of love, they sing "For love is as strong as death, its jealousy

unyielding as the grave. It burns like blazing fire, like a mighty f lame". Jacob was in love with Rachel so he told her father, "I'll work for you seven years in return for your younger daughter Rachel". Rachel's father agreed. So Jacob served seven years to get Rachel, but they seemed like only a few days to him because of his love for her. Another example of first love can be found in the story of Esther. The king was attracted to Esther more than to any of the other women, and she won his favor and approval more than any of the other virgins. He set a royal crown on her head and made her queen instead of Vashti. Esther became a powerless sex partner to a king who strongly preferred women who never interfered with his wishes. She came only when he call. And when she courageously went when he did not call: when he saw her his love for her was stirred within. So he held out to her his gold scepter and told her whatever is your request, I'll give it to you, even if it is half the kingdom. So girls to have love in a marriage is a very, very important quality because when all else fails <u>love</u> never fails.

LESSON 3

LIVING A FULFILLED SINGLE LIFE

I Corinthians 7: 7b – God gives some the gift of marriage,
and to others he gives the gift of singleness. NLT

I. Fulfilled Only in Christ

    A. Through Salvation (II Corinthians 5: 17)

    B. Growing in Grace (II Corinthians 9: 8)

    C. Trusting in Jesus (Psalms 37: 3-5)

    D. Walking in the Spirit (Galatians 5: 16-26)

II. Fulfilled by Accepting Your Proper Gift

    A. The Single

    1. Serve God Better (I Corinthians 7: 34-35)

    2. Careth for Things that Belong to God. (I Corinthians 7: 25-32)

    B. The Married

    1. Held in Honor (Hebrews 13: 4)

    2. Ordained of God (Genesis 2: 18-25)

    3. Prevent Irregular Affection (I Corinthians 7: 9)

    4. Indeed a Blessing (Proverbs 5: 18)

    5. Careth for the Things of this World (I Corinthians 7: 33)

III. Fulfilled Through Patience (Hebrews 10: 36; Psalms 37:7; Romans 12: 12)

LIVING A FULFILLED SINGLE LIFE

I Corinthians 7: 7b – God gives some the gift of marriage,
and to others he gives the gift of singleness. NLT

I. Introduction

If a man would stay single, he'd save himself a lots of grief. As terrible as this statement may sound, it accurately, if only partially ref lects Jesus teaching on the subject. In Matt. 19: 11, Jesus agreed with his disciples that "it is better not to marry", and as he replied, "not everyone can accept that, but only those to whom it has been given". Then Jesus revealed what he meant by describing the various kinds of eunuchs in verse 12. But let's look at that statement again, "not everyone can accept that, but only those to whom it has been given". In other words, if a man can accept the idea that the single state is better having no necessity sexually for marriage, he should stay single, because most men and women have sex drives that demands fulfillment . In the book of the I Corinthians Paul gives advice to a church composed of converted idolaters, adulterers, prostitutes, thieves, drunkards, and swindlers. Paul tries to convince these people of the immorality of sexual activities that had been a part of everyday worship under their old religion. Paul expresses his response to the single life in the 7th chapter of Corinthians. He carefully distinguishes what is his personal opinion and what is a clear revelation from God. He explains explicitly in each verse why he reached these conclusions. Not every breakdown in Corinth will recur in churches today, but Paul's principles can apply to our own unpredictable experience that we may encounters during our single life. Let us prayerfully and devotionally examine these principles.

II. Fulfilled Only in Christ

Imagine a college freshman standing in a corridor amidst a swirl of chattering students. In two minutes the next class will begin. But for her, time has stopped. She has just opened a tear-stained, 12 page letter from her parents. The tone of the letter takes her by surprise. Her parents are normally reserved not given to emotional outbursts. Their letters are usually warm and friendly. Not this time, somehow they have heard about her recent behavior on campus, and they are very hurt. In a torrent of words, they pour out their feelings for her and their equally deep disappointments. Their letter may have went something like this:

Dear Harriet and John:

Your father and I are writing this letter not to shame you but to warn you as our dear children about your conduct and behavior as Christians while you are in college. Remember to let your light shine. Be an example, let your peers see the newness of life that they can live as a new creation in Christ Jesus…remember to let your light shine. Live by the word and give the word to your new friends and classmates as often as it is needed. Stay in prayer. Let God's grace sustain you and may his words be a lamp unto your feet…now you know John going to that gay bar with those other boys….Harriet I was shocked to hear that my little girl was caught necking and petting on a public bench on the campus grounds. You may think that you are having fun. Well just let me tell you something. You haven't had fun until you totally submit yourselves to God, and commit your way unto him. Shall we come to visit you with a whip or in love and with a gentle spirit? It is better to repent and confess your sins than to continue in your sins and lose your souls to hell fire. We love you John and Harriet…Resist the devil. Live by the Spirit and you will not want to gratify the desires of the sinful nature…When we visit you we want to pray with you…we are fasting for you…I know that if you will heed our warnings you will experience true fulfillment and happiness in Christ Jesus….

QUESTIONS:

1. How do you react when someone --- a parent, a teacher, boss, or pastor --- tries to straighten you out?
2. Do the qualities of life in the spirit listed in Galatians 5: 22-23, characterize your life?
3. Do you think John and Harriet parents' letter was a help to them?

III. Fulfilled by Accepting Your Proper Gift

A. The Single

In a society where marriages are breaking up all around, Christian singles often wonder whether it is perhaps better not to enter marriage. Yet single Christians find the going extremely tough. Temptations are f lung at them from the media, from advertising, from the life-styles of friends and relatives. Even sexual perversions can exert a strong pull. Some people are still called to the single Christian life in our day, but the ability to succeed in it is definitely in the 7th chapter of I Corinthians. Since Christians were facing great dangers to their lives during that time, Paul felt that it was better for a person to not marry. But if you do marry during these times, it is no sin. However, marriage will bring about extra problems that Paul did not want the Corinthians couples to face. In all you do Paul says to the Corinthians I want you to be free from worry but if you get married you will have earthly responsibilities. An unmarried man can spend his time doing the Lord's work and thinking about how to please him. Paul tells the Corinthians that he is saying this to not keep him from marrying, but he wants them to do whatever will help them to serve the Lord best, with as few other things as possible to distract their attention from God. So neither the single nor the married state is "better". We should accept the state to which God calls us.

QUESTIONS:

    1. Why did Paul say that the single can serve God better than the married?

    2. Upon what should a Christian base the decision of whether to marry or to remain single?

    3. How can churches support those who believe they have the gift of celibacy?

B. The Married

Innumerable forces work against a secure and healthy marriage. Is there hope for Christians trying to maintain such a marriage? Yes, there is even if you live in an immoral neighborhood or are confronted with unfavorable circumstances in society. Christ's power and authority goes to unfavorable circumstances and immoral settings to prove that Jesus is still at work in the heart and soul of men.

For marriage is honorable. It is ordained of God. It prevents irregular affections and it is indeed a blessing. Believers today, whether married or single, have the opportunity to please God by living faithfully the life-style to which he has called them. For every man hath his proper gift of God, the gift to remain single or the gift to marry. Seek God prayerfully about yours.

QUESTIONS:

    1. Does anyone know their proper gift of God?

    2. Can a Christian couple be a light in an immoral neighborhood?

IV. Fulfilled Through Patience

James says that the testing of one's faith worketh patience. Patience is steadfast endurance. A single Christian can find true contentment and fulfillment by exemplifying patience through expectation. What this mean is that if you have done God's will then you can look for God to keep his promise that he has made to you. We can rejoice in the hope of our promise. And remember to keep praying while you're patiently waiting. Rest in the Lord, and don't fret and worry about evil men who prosper. God lets us know that the wicked shall disappear, but all who humble themselves before the Lord, and wait patiently on God, shall be given every blessing, and shall have wonderful peace.

QUESTIONS:

1. What do you usually do when you're frustrated and worried?
2. Patience in temptation shows maturity. Never rush an answer. This is easier said sometimes than done. Would anyone like to share an impatient experience and its result?

LESSON 4

WHAT'S THE APPROPRIATE OUTLET?

I Corinthians 6: 20 – for God bought you with a high price.
So you must honor God with your body. NLT

I. Introduction

II. Drugs (Proverbs 23: 29-33; Proverbs 20: 1; I Corinthians 3: 16-17)

    A. Harmful effects
    B. Reasons Teenagers take Drugs
    C. How to Use Drugs Safely

III. Sex (I Corinthians 5: 1; Leviticus 18: 5-24)

IV. Satanic Worship (Acts 15: 29; I Corinthians 10: 20-22; Deuteronomy 18: 9-12; Acts 19: 19-20)

V. Rock Music (Deuteronomy 7: 26; Ephesians 5: 8-20; Colossians 3: 16)

WHAT'S THE APPROPRIATE OUTLET

I Corinthians 6: 20 – for God bought you with a high price.
So you must honor God with your body. NLT

I. Introduction

The main cause of the rise in death rate for the age group 15-24 years old as reported by the Surgeon General in 1985 is driving mixed with substances. What are substances? That's the name often given to alcohol and drugs. Further evidence of how dangerous these chemicals can be is that the 2nd reason for deaths in this age group is alcohol---and drug related suicides and accidents that don't involve driving. Dr. Paul King of Charter Lakeside hospital believe that drugs and rock music especially heavy metal music is the cause of most violent behavior in teenagers. Six out of 10 Memphis area youths treated for alcohol and drug problems at a Memphis psychiatric hospital was deeply influenced by heavy metal rock music. The sexual violence, satanic and suicidal messages in heavy metal music do not in themselves cause teenagers to drink or take drugs but Paul King believe that it contributes to teenage drug abuse, and teenage rebellion. In this lesson I hope that each of us will better come to terms with what's a good outlet or release for Christian young adults and what are wrong outlets. We want to look at what God has to say about Drugs, Sex, Satanic Worship and Rock Music. After this let's pray for God to keep us from evils, as we endeavor to keep our minds staying on praises.

II. Drugs

"Just Say No", is a familiar phrase to many American who are concerned about the increasing use of illicit drugs by our youths. Most reasons teenagers give for using drugs are: it changes my feelings; it solves my problems; peer pressures, etc.. Everyone sometimes have bad feelings or problems that make them feel uncomfortable and I'm sure that all of us

at one time or another has felt pressured to do the same as others because we wanted to be accepted, or belong, or be a part of a group. To be saved often means that sometimes you cannot go along with the crowd. You must be an example of the believer in word, conduct, and action. Somebody wants to know Jesus can you show them Jesus through your lifestyle as well as tell them about him. I have listed below terms for the drugs, alcohol, and nicotine. Let's take a brief look at those terms and then let's look at the handout on Getting Help for more information on drugs.(see the index at end of this book)

1. Alcohol: A colorless f lammable liquid, obtained by fermentation of sugars and starches and used as a solvent in drugs, and in intoxicating beverages; ethanol.[5]
2. Nicotine: A colorless poisonous alkaloid, derived from the tobacco plant and used as an insecticide.[6]

People who can help young adults with drug problems includes:

1. A A(Alcoholic Anonymous) – A group to help the family or close friends of alcoholics
2. Mental Health Centers – Provides counselors who talk to drug users and their families about drug abuse; they help drug users to stop using drugs.
3. Church – A minister or counselor can provide personal help by talking about drug problem.

Remember that medicine is for people who are ill and should be only used according to specific rules. It should be taken at the right time and in the proper amount. When we follow those rules we are using drugs not abusively but in a safe and protective way.

---

5 The American Heritage Dictionary, 4th ed., (Massachusetts: Houghton Miff lin Company, 2001), 21.
6 Ibid., 573

III. Sex

In our previous lessons we have discussed various sexual sins such as fornication, lasciviousness and homosexuality. However, we have not discussed the sexual perversion of incest. Incest is sexual intercourse between persons so closely related that marriage is illegal. In the 5th chapter of Corinthians Paul wanted the Corinthians to expel a brother in the church who was sleeping with his mother. Paul stresses that this will perhaps teach the offender a lesson. For if he is handed over to satan as Paul states which means to be put out, then maybe this person sinful life he's living in the flesh which is incest can possibly be destroyed and his spirit saved at a later time on the Lord's Day. In the book of Leviticus, the 18th chapter, God's warning against various sexual practices like incest begins and ends with warnings to the Israelites to be more differently from their neighbors. I just want to encourage you to keep in mind that God has not called us unto uncleanness but unto holiness, and remember the wrong kind of sex that is unpleasing to God brings agony, but if we follow God's laws and doctrines that pertains to sex than we know that sex can bring ecstasy.

IV. Satanic Worship

Teenagers around the country are dabbling in devil worship as a vent for anti-establishment feelings said psychiastrists contacted by one new reporter. Some of you are in college or who will be going to college will encounter these young Satanists. Some of you who may have been blessed to go through school without being approached by a group such as this may on your new jobs meet for the first time someone who is participating in occult practices and rituals. These Satanists blend well into society for they take on the appearances of an average working class citizen. Dr. Richard Evans, a University of Houston social psychologist said teens can be attracted to any kind of cult if they have a "self esteem vacuum" and are seeking identity and social acceptance. Satanism which revels in evil, destruction, instant gratification and rituals guaranteed to shock parents offers the ultimate

rebellion of young teens. Signs to look for in a young adult who is dabbling into the occult are: school grades dropping drastically; more isolation from family members; aggressive and angry behavior; they began to wear inverted crosses, encircled pentagrams, goat heads, the number 666 as jewelry or drawings on notebooks; they may began to wear more black clothing than before.

Engaging in the occults brings fear and confusion in one's life. The longer one remains in it the more damage Satan does to the psyche of man. Cannibalism is Satanism in its worst stage. An incident of cannibalism was reported in the Sur area in California in 1973. A man was picked up and taken to the police department. When they examined his pockets they found human parts that he carried around eating on. Satan knows that his end is near, so he's pushing witchcraft as hard as he can. His organization has an endless supply of money. Movies like Jesus Christ superstar, and GodSpell came depicting Jesus as a loser and a clown. There are many people who don't read their Bibles so they believe the movies. The Exorcist also pictured Satan as winning. The film shows Jesus powerless against the devil, but we know who wins in the end. Satan must get permission from God before he can make a move against a true Christian believer (Job 1: 6-12). Young people put on the whole armour of God, that you may be able to stand against the wiles of the devils. For we wrestle not against f lesh and blood, but against powers, against the rulers of the darkness of this world against spiritual wickedness in high places. Put your angels around you as you go out each day and trust in the Lord. Have faith in God. Take him at his word and stand on his promises.

V. Rock Music

Illicit sex, the drug culture, witchcraft and rock music go hand in hand. How many hundreds of thousands, even millions of young people have started out on the road to drugs because their "gods" of rock and roll set the example? One can't help but wonder how much further it can go, but one does know where it's leading. This road is characterized by a wasted life that will culminate in an early and tragic death. Rock and Roll as it has degenerated into punk rock and new wave, has played a major role in promoting suicide through the lie that suicide is the logical answer since life is without hope. It started with Elvis, Jerry Lee and the Beatles. This was followed by hard rock and acid rock, and now we are subjected to punk rock. Rock music represents a rebellion against all authority, and its source is confirmed by the dress, bizarre hair coloration, and markings (mutilation) of the bodies of its followers.

Music should encourage and lift the soul. It should bring a ray of sunshine into the heart that is discouraged by the pressures of the day. Of course, I'm speaking of true Gospel music which is sacred and uplifting. God can use Christian music to touch the hearts and lives of both the saved and unsaved. Music should refresh the spirit and glorify God. Rock music is associated with the music the Druids used during their occult ceremony. The instruments they used were a flute, a tambourine and a drum covered with human hide. The words to every song or melody were for casting spell. The drum beat was the key to addict the listener. It is a form of hypnotism. The same beat the druids used is in the rock music of today, both hard rock and soft rock.

One of the greatest victories in the occult world was to penetrate the "Christian" music with Satanic beats. Christian children who've destroyed their rock records were pulled back to worldly rock music again after listening to "Christian Rock". The most powerful spells hitting Christian homes come through rock music that's why when young people get saved they should burn all their rock records if they have any. These records contain coded spells or incantations put there by witches. Every recording that has been blessed by witches has a visitor (demon) with it. That's why some homes are so messed up.

Parents allow the spell to be put on their home when they allow their child to listen to such music. Below are steps every Christian must take to block Satan's attack and to be free from the spells of rock music.

1. Clean out your homes of occult objects.
2. Make Jesus Lord of every part of your life.
3. Read your Bible faithfully everyday.
4. In prayer, reject occult involvement in the past. Plead the blood of Jesus for protection and bind the demonic forces.
5. Submit yourselves to God, resist the devil and he'll f lee from you.

BIBLIOGRAPHY

American Heritage Dictionary. Massachusetts: Houghton Miff lin Company, 2001.

Brosnan, James W. "Heavy Metal Attacked in study of Drug Abusers."
    The Commercial Appeal 148th year No. 429, 4 sections, Memphis, TN,
    Tuesday Morning, October 27, 1987.

Chick, Jack T. The Broken Cross. 1974, P. O. Box 662, Chino
California 19710, U.S.A. published by Chick Publications, 1974.

Rothenberg, M.D., Mikel A. and C. F. Chapman. "Syphilis; Gonorrhea; Aids;
HIV". Dictionary of Medical Terms. Barron's Education Series Inc., 1989.

LESSON PLANS AND ACTIVITY SHEETS

SUGGESTED LESSON PLAN FOR LESSON 1

TITLE: "ABSTINENCE, MARRIAGE and ETC. …"

SUB-TITLE: The Agony

MEMORY VERSE: God hath not called us unto uncleanness but unto holiness.

I Thessalonians 4: 7 KJV

OBJECTIVE: That students will take care in crucial choices that concern love, sex and marriage.

PROCEDURES:

 STEP 1: The teacher will present lesson by giving a brief synopsis (in your own way) on its topic, lesson, objective and outline.

 STEP 2: Students may read the scripture passages for Lesson 1 of outline. Afterwards, let students read through lesson's introduction and outline I I, subject matter.

 STEP 3: Ask your own discussion questions. Allow one minute for comments from students or parents. (Complete Outline III, IV and V the same as above)

 STEP 4: Shortly before dismissal take another look at The objective. Let students express the decision they have acquired from this lesson. Closing by praying that the Godly commitment they have acquired may be sustained in all their decisions about love sex and marriage.

If you have planned a tea or buffet the lesson will last quite possibly two hours. Do not rush the lesson. It would be most appropriate to serve the meals before the lesson or after the lesson. Keep in mind the lesson is the most important event.

SUGGESTED LESSON PLAN FOR LESSON 2

TITLE: "ABSTINENCE, MARRIAGE and ETC. …"

SUB-TITLE: The Ecstasy

MEMORY VERSE: God hath not called us unto uncleanness but unto holiness.

I Thessalonians 4:7 KJV

OBJECTIVE: That Students will take care in crucial choices that concern love, sex, and marriage.

PROCEDURES

STEP 1: Give each student a partner. Give partners one minute to socialize using the Alpha activity (see worksheet at the end of this plan). After a minute ask the students, "How do you feel?" Their response indicate the way their partner made them feel. Let students know that they can start a friendship this way.

STEP 2: Say, "A friendship can develop into love, and we know love leads to marriage". Let students complete the readings for this topic. Use your own discussion starters. (complete the other part of the outline in the same way.)

STEP 3: Close the lesson with prayer. A questionnaire that allows students to express their views about dating, love, sex, etc., is most helpful. I have a copy of one that you can use or you can make your own. Suggested teaching aids: books, or articles that relate to your topic; Bibles, pamphlets, etc.

ALPHA ACTIVITY -- Find Someone In The Group Who:

1._____Has the name of a male Bible character.

2._____Has the name of a female Bible character.

3._____Can say the Lord's Prayer…..

4._____Can quote Psalm 23….

5._____Can name six of the apostles…….

6._____Can name six of the twelve tribes.

7._____Has a mother with a Bible name.

8._____Has a father with a Bible name.

9._____Can name the first three Kings of Israel.

10._____Can name the first and last book of the Bible.

11._____Knows Jesus' Forerunner.

12._____Knows who wrote most of the Epistles.

13._____Has a sister with a Bible name.

14._____Has a brother with a Bible name.

15._____Knows their pastor's name.

QUESTIONNAIRE

1. Should a person kiss on the first date?
2. Is petting wrong?
3. What is the difference between love and lust?
4. What is the appropriate age for dating?
5. Should a Christian engage in homosexuality?
6. As a Christian I believe that sex is for married couples. However, is it wrong to masturbate?
7. Where should Christians go on a date?
8. Should I have sex if I think about it?
9. Should Christians write love letter?
10. How can one deal with peer pressures to not engage in sex?

SUGGESTED LESSON PLAN FOR LESSON 3

TITLE: "Living a Fulfilled Single Life"

MEMORY VERSE: …God gives some the gift of marriage, and to others he gives the gift of singleness. I Corinthians 7: 7b

OBJECTIVE: That youths will receive information about the fulfilling joy of living single.

PROCEDURES:

 STEP 1: The teacher will present lesson by giving a brief synopsis (in your own way) on the lesson's topic, lesson's objective and outline. (be real)

 STEP 2: Students will read the scripture passages for part I of the outline. Afterwards, let students read through lesson introduction and outline II subject matter.

 STEP 3: Allow one minute for comments from students or parents for discussing the questions after the lesson.

 STEP 4: Review your objective. Let students express their committed decisions from this lesson. Closing by praying that the youth will be given guidance about their single state.

SUGGESTED LESSON PLAN FOR LESSON 4

TITLE: "What's The Appropriate Outlet?"

MEMORY VERSE: …for God bought you with a high price. So you musthonor God with your body. I Corinthians 6: 20

OBJECTIVE: That your students will gain confidence in Christ's power and will bring their spiritual and physical needs to him.

PROCEDURES

 STEP 1: Teacher will ask students "What is your hobby?" (wait for responses) Introduce topic, memory verse and objective after students responses. Inform students that the lesson will help them to answer the topic's question. The teacher will say, "The lesson is informative, enlightening, and is helpful in making practical decisions".

 STEP 2: The teacher will let students read the scriptures in outline I. After scriptures reading let students read the introduction and outline I readings. If you have health agencies pamphlets to give, now would be appropriate. A resource person would be appropriate now too, or a dvd about drugs.

 STEPS 3: Ask your own discussion questions after the resource person. Allow 1 minute for comments.

 STEP 4: Keeping your objective in mind, close by praying that the students will make sensible spiritual and physical goals and dreams for themselves.

Suggested teaching aids: a resource person, health agencies, pamphlets, etc.

GETTING HELP

INCEST-----Anyone who suspects that a child is being sexually abused should call the district attorney's office, the sex crimes unit of their local police department, a local child welfare agency, or the national child sexual abuse hotline: 1-800-422-4453.

The following national organization can also provide information and guidance on resources in local communities:

CLEARINGHOUSE ON CHILD ABUSE AND NEGLECT INFORMATION

P. O. BOX 1182

WASHINGTON, D. C. 20013

1-301-251-5157

D. HENRY KEMPE NATIONAL CENTER FOR PREVENTION OF CHILD ABUSE AND NEGLECT

1205 ONEIDA STREET

DENVER, COLOR ADO 80220

1-303-321-3963

NATIONAL CENTER ON CHILD ABUSE AND NEGLECT ADMINISTRATION FOR CHILDREN, YOUTH, AND FAMILIES DEPARTMENT OF HEALTH AND HUMAN SERVICES

P. O. BOX 1182

WASHINTON, D. C. 20013

1-202-245-2859

PARENTS ANONYMOUS

22330 HAWTHORNE BOULEVARD, SUITE 208

TORR ANCE, CALIFORNIA 90505

1-213-371-3501

PARENTS UNITED

P. O. BOX 952

SAN JOSE, CALIFORNIA 95108

1-408-280-5055

1-800-241-9746 -- PRIDE Drug Information Line

1-800-638-2045 – National Institute On Drug Abuse (NIDA)

U. S. Department of Health and Human Services

ABOUT THE AUTHOR

Missionary Faith Bays has a nursing home ministry in her community. She is also a prolific speaker in her hometown church, the Church of God in Christ. This is Faith's second publishing of her book. It has a new title: *Abstinence, Marriage, Etc. ...*Faith received a Master of Divinity from Liberty University in 2019. She is currently working on a Doctor of Ministry at Liberty. She hopes to purse a Phd after completing her doctoral work at Liberty.

This book is of course about abstinence, marriage and other topics for the youths. It is Faith's desire that the young people as well as the young in heart will enjoy her book and it will bless you spiritually. Faith also asks that you will pray for her ministry if you are enjoying its blessings.

Printed in the United States
By Bookmasters